Authenticity Matters

A Guide to Purpose, Power, and Possibility.

C. Simone Rivers

Pearly Gates Publishing LLC
P.O. Box 62287
Houston, TX 77205

Authenticity Matters
A Guide to Purpose, Power, and Possibility

Copyright © 2017
C. Simone Rivers

All Rights Reserved.
No portion of this publication may be reproduced, stored in any electronic system, or transmitted in any form or by any means (electronic, mechanical, photocopy, recording, or otherwise) without written permission from the publisher. Brief quotations may be used in literary reviews.

Scriptures are used by permission from Zondervan via Biblegateway.com.

ISBN 10: 1945117788
ISBN 13: 978-1945117787
Library of Congress Control Number:
2017944615

For information and bulk ordering, contact:
Pearly Gates Publishing LLC
Angela R. Edwards, CEO
P.O. Box 62287
Houston, TX 77205
BestSeller@PearlyGatesPublishing.com

DEDICATION

To my amazing man, Victor, and my handsome sons, Joshua and Jameson, thank you for every story we wrote together that led to this moment. I love you.

This book is dedicated to the memory of Rev. Dr. Arthur T. Jones, Harrison Goddard, and Ricky Thomas. You each have taught me that impossible really is a lie!

INTRODUCTION

I believe there are no coincidences in life. It is not by happenstance that this book was brought to your awareness or that you are reading it right now. There is a reason for this particular connection at this specific moment in time. I call it "divine intersection"—spiritually orchestrated paths crossing day in and day out.

The thing I've found interesting is that we don't always pay attention to those intersections—those souls who cross our paths from day to day. We don't pay attention to what they might be carrying just for us. Quite frankly, we ignore a lot!

How many times has someone asked how you were, and you responded with a random thought like, "Thank you! You, too!"? You were not listening to that person at all. Your conversation was with yourself, or perhaps some past thought or future hope, but you were not present.

However, there are those times when our Spirit reminds us that our specific personalities are absolutely necessary. The individuals that we are—we are necessary. Our authentic selves matter!

I want to share a story with you that was a sort of impetus and lifeblood for this book. For those of you battling with self-esteem, self-value, or self-identity, just keep reading. I believe this will change your life, as it showed up in my experience and changed me.

I want you to know that you are special. You have been designed by the Divine with a specific narrative that only you can convey to the world. If you don't fit the description of one who battles in those areas listed above, are you masking your truth with the perception of power? Are you continuing to be who others say you should be versus who you really are or really want to be?

I would like to introduce you to a path that will lead you to who you were meant to be.

Doesn't everyone really want to be themselves? It is exhausting keeping up with the stories we tell the world about who we are. My mom used to say, "Baby, if you don't lie, you don't have to remember so much". The masks get heavy. I am a living witness to the fact that authenticity breeds peace — a peace that surpasses all understanding.

****

I lived in Europe for more than a decade and had some awesome intersections with the divinity of other people.

One particular instance, I was "people-watching" while in a mall in Germany (something I really enjoy doing). There was this woman trying to find something to wear on what I thought was a date. She seemed incredibly frustrated. So, being my normal, deliciously-fabulous self, I asked if I could help. She appeared genuinely happy for the attention, and I was overjoyed to offer it. We became best friends for about two and a half hours! I found outfit after outfit for her to try on, and she bought several of them. I even gifted her some accessories just to bless her forward. It was so much fun!

We parted ways with a hug and "Gotte segne dich" ("God bless you" in German). I never got her name and don't recall giving her mine.

That didn't matter. It was just a normal day for me. It's who I am. It's what I do. It's my personality expressing itself.

I had no idea she was describing me to people in our community and trying to find me…

A few weeks later, I received a phone call. The person on the other end of the line introduced herself as "Silke" and began to remind me of how we met in the mall.

"Ja. Ja. Wie geht es dir? I remember. Did you find a place to wear your new clothes?"

She paused for a moment, and what she shared next is something I will never forget. She wanted to thank me for being kind to her and making her laugh that day. She said I had no idea how despondent she really was.

You see, Silke had just lost her only son in an accident on the autobahn a few days prior to our encounter in the mall. She felt like life was over for her as well. She couldn't find any reasons for waking up in the morning. That day, she was shopping for what she wanted people to find her in when they found her body.

I gasped inside, but I didn't speak. I just listened as tears began to roll down my face.

What I know is that I have worn every mask you can imagine in my life, trying to make myself fit in to what others said I should be. I dimmed my light just a little because others thought it was too bright. I shrank so others could feel bigger around me.

But, on that day, in that store, with that stranger, I was the most authentic I had ever been. We giggled, shopped, and had a big, old, loud, bright good time! Just that simple expression of who I truly am saved her life. I was overwhelmed! I remain overwhelmed knowing that God desires to change a few of my behaviors, but finds my personality absolutely necessary!

I'm saying to you right now, as you turn the pages of this book, you are more than enough. You are absolutely necessary!

Who you are matters.

Who I am matters.

Puppets are the expressions of others. Their strings are being pulled to create movement, versus their independent movement in the world, which (in my view) is a key part of being authentic. When you embrace the energy of your true self, there is a power you tap into. There is the opportunity to maximize your life's potential as you discover your real purpose. And, there are even people who organically find you and make your experience so much better. They begin to fan the sparks of possibility and create a raging fire of significance.

Don't look for this book to be some complicated approach to an esoteric life. Authenticity has become esoteric, I think, because we have lost sight of the fact that we are enough.

Perhaps my hair is shorter than hers; but my hair, for me, is enough. Perhaps my home is larger or smaller than the next; but my home is enough, and its size absolutely necessary for my life.

It's in the comparison game that we find fault in who we are intended and purposed to be, and we connect and find a need to be someone or something else. The advent of social media has made this phenomenon multiply exponentially. What we seem to disconnect from is this truth. People only post the best of their lives on social media. They show you the new baby, but they don't share the dirty diapers, sleepless nights, or fear of not being able to feed the child. They post their new car photos, but neglect to share how much the car note is and just how much they had to sacrifice to get it.

The point is, you can't compare your worst day to someone else's best and call it fair! In fact, all comparison starts out unfair. You have not equal. We are all unique expressions of a loving Creator.

I make a daily practice of "turning off". I turn off my computer, my phone, log out of social media, and I sit in silence. Some call it meditation. That's fine, but I prefer to call it sitting in silence because I've never really understood how to meditate. This ignorance created a space for me to compare myself to those who can, like Deepak

Chopra. Yes, I compared my meditation ability to the guru himself! I told you that comparing is unfair! How do you think I know? Because I have done it, too.

What I chose to do is just be quiet for a while every day and allow inspiration to speak to me and guide me. I used to be so afraid to do this. Silence was deafening to me at one time in my life! I needed noise—or so I thought. When I allowed myself to actually listen to the silence, I heard the most beautiful sound; the sound of my own Voice, my Source, my Spirit, God. It offered me comfort in the midst of the chaos of my life. It offered me a knowing that I want to share with the world. I know for sure that who I am is exactly who I was meant to be, and without a single doubt, I am enough. I have enough. I will always be enough.

Defining Authenticity

What exactly is authenticity? I define authenticity as the closest version to the truth of who you are and who you were meant to be. It's accuracy, truth, and fidelity to who you really are. Sometimes, we need help finding our true selves because there are layers and layers of masks we've found to protect that vulnerable person.

Don't be upset with yourself because you still have masks. Our brains are wired to protect us, to build mechanisms to guard us from hurt, harm, and danger. It makes sense that we would have masks. Some of our brains even create stories to help us cope with our reality.

When I was a very young girl, I created a story about my father. I told everyone who would listen that my father died when I was 12 years old. As I grew into my teen years and early into college, that story grew legs that carried me.

My father died when I was 12. He named me after Nina Simone because he had seen her in France.

I told the story so well, I actually believed it! It helped me survive the truth that I was not equipped to face at such a young age. The truth is father passed away when I was just four years old. The story I created gave me the love of my dad and allowed me to grow up experiencing that love. I was in my early 30s when I ran across his death certificate in my mom's house. At that age, even though it was extremely painful for me, I was able to handle the truth of his death and accept that I had created his life to care for the four-year-old me.

So, don't beat yourself up for carrying your bag of masks. I get it. This book is offered to help you unpack your bags and show the world YOU!

<u>H</u>ello <u>E</u>ternal <u>L</u>oving <u>P</u>resence

That is what "HELP" is—a greeting and acknowledgment of the eternal, loving presence of God. I snatched this concept from Michael Bernard Beckwith. I think it is an awesome example of the place from which all of our help comes. Asking for help is a prayer. So, for those of you asking how to find and live in your authenticity, that's my answer, **HELP!**

I'm living in my purpose by offering help in the pages of this book.

This book will guide you to the knowing that you are enough. You have enough. You will always be enough. Oh yeah, and you are necessary!

TABLE OF CONTENTS

DEDICATION VI
INTRODUCTION VII
DON'T FIGHT THE POWER 1
LET IT SHINE 13
CAN YOU HEAR ME NOW? 21
TAKE IT ALL OFF! 29
LINKED IN 37
SHE CAN'T READ 47
IN LIVING COLOR 55
LIFELINE 61
EPILOGUE 71
ACKNOWLEDGMENTS 78
WHAT OTHERS ARE SAYING… 80
ABOUT THE AUTHOR 83

Don't Fight the Power

"The power of your authenticity offers access to every desire tattooed on your soul."

~ C. Simone Rivers ~

Often, I hear people use words that are commonsensical for most of the world, but I just feel like I can't relate. POWER is one of those words. I've always either been trying to get some or increase what I thought I had, only to discover I never had it in the first place.

Is that confusing? Well, let me explain.

I grew up in a small town called Eatonville in the central part of Florida, about six miles north of Orlando. My family moved there when I was seven years old. This is the earliest memory I have of a home and what it looked like. My father passed away, leaving my mom alone with six children. She bought a home for us in Eatonville. It was an African-American town. In fact, it is an historical town where Zora Neale Hurston shared herself during the Renaissance, and it was the very first African-American incorporated town in the United States.

We lived at the end of a dirt road and had orange groves across from us and to the right of our house. When I was seven, I remember having a telephone and talking to a boy down the street who I thought I was madly in love with at the ripe, old age of seven!

I remember having electricity in the house, taking baths at night before bed, and brushing my teeth in the morning before school. However, that is the only time I recall those things being in place, when I was seven.

I also remember having no telephone and being the object of ridicule and mean-spirited comments from the kids in my school because we didn't have a working phone line in our home.

I also remember being really careful with a kerosene lamp that sat on the windowsill as I did my homework and read books because I didn't have electricity.

I remember taking a big, white bucket to my next-door neighbor's house, filling it with water twice a day to pour into our toilet so that it would flush, because our water had been shut off. I remember brushing my teeth with toothpaste and rinsing when I got to school.

I remember feeling completely powerless when I looked at how hard my mom worked to take care of us.

I remember being the only African-American child in my school, Northside Christian Academy. I remember the white school van picking me up from my house every morning, then going to pick up my schoolmates in different neighborhoods with huge houses, palm trees, and beautiful grass. I knew they had water because the sprinklers were always on, every morning. Our house didn't look like theirs, and my powerlessness continued to increase.

I remember the uniforms we wore: white button-up, collared, short-sleeved shirt, and A-line navy-blue skirt, white socks, and oxford saddle shoes. My mom would always put a red bow in my hair. I loved my uniform because it was just like my peers'. It gave me a feeling of belonging. There was a certain power in belonging for me. Wearing that uniform made me feel smarter and more capable.

I remember how proud my mother was when I got my report card from my teachers. I could affect her smile, and that made me feel powerful. So, I did my very best in school.

I remember going back to a public school and losing that powerful feeling all over again. I didn't have the clothes my schoolmates had because we didn't have the resources their families had. There were so many rich kids at my school. But I was smart. I could still do *something*, so I did!

When high school came around, I took advanced placement classes and heard from my counselors that I could get scholarships to go to college if I did my best in those classes. I didn't understand what was being said to me, but what I did know was that doing my best would affect some kind of change.

As a child, I think I spent almost as much time in church as I did in school. I can't remember which preacher said it, but I know now that he was quoting Dr. Martin Luther King when he did. He said the definition of power was "the ability to effect change" and that God was the source of our power, but He gave us access to it. That resonated with me in a profound way. As long as I could effect change in some way—big or small—I had power!

So, what does that have to do with authenticity? I'm glad you asked!

We are all plugged into the Source. It doesn't matter a whole lot to me what you call your Source—God, Yahweh, Buddha... Just knowing we are all plugged into the Source is the point I want you to pick up and carry with you.

This is the source of our power—our "Power Source", if you will.

We have access to great power; however, we cannot tap into that power if we are not our authentic selves. The magnitude of our power depends on the efficiency of our 'appliances'.

Let me paint the picture for you: When my family moved to Europe, we brought with us some electronics we owned in the states, thinking that we would be able to continue to use them. We found out the hard way that it just wasn't the case. We had to buy transformers that converted the devices made in North America to ones that could be used in Europe. While the devices did convert the voltage to one that would work, it did not offer the same level of power.

When I used a converter for my blender, it didn't blend as well. When I used a converter for my lamp, the light wasn't as bright. BUT when I took the same lamp and plugged it into the correct power source, I got the maximum brightness from the wattage of the bulb that I expected.

When we mask our true selves, we decrease our access to the 'Power Source', and we aren't as bright as we could be. We aren't as strong as we could be. We aren't able to blend the pieces of our lives together as well as they could be. BUT when we operate within the framework of our own authenticity, we access a power that can truly effect change — change in our physical selves, our spiritual selves, our emotional selves — truly every part of ourselves! THAT is what real personal power looks like.

So, masks down! Power up!

More about that power...

"There is a hunger inside of people to express themselves creatively and feel authentic doing it."
~ Sean Penn ~

My first memory of knowing that I am creative was in junior high school (that's middle school in the modern age). I was in the sixth grade, and my English teacher, Ms. Gwinn, required that we write a short story for an early elementary school audience. The best stories would be chosen and read to the elementary school students.

The story I wrote was titled *The Valentine Family*. It was about this family of Valentine cards that were still on the shelf on February 15th. The story started out rather sad but had a happy ending, letting everyone know that their usefulness would be discovered by the world.

I actually won the "contest" and was allowed to read my story to the elementary school. Ms. Gwinn referred to me as a "creative spirit". I remember clinging to those words like life itself. Her words offered me evidence that I had been looking for to describe what I had always known about myself. From that moment on, I've called myself a 'Creative Spirit'. I identified with her words in my very being.

I write. I used words as an art form, with paper as my canvas and the pen, my brush. That has always sounded so lofty to me and gave me a real sense of pride saying it. It's true, but it is not true for just me! It's true for all of us! Creativity exists in every one of us. We have the power to produce from just our thinking. When we are our authentic selves, we are able to access the power of our creativity. The really interesting part of it is that we don't *have* to access it. We can deny it, just as we deny our own truth every day when we put on those masks.

Academics tend to deny creativity because it is immeasurable in their world, but unused or denied, creativity does not disappear. It is not considerate. It is not compassionate. It doesn't wait for you to decide to use it and somehow becomes gracious or understanding. Oh no! Creativity that has been denied becomes a cancer on your soul. It hurts. It bites. It claws. It scratches and refuses to go silently into the night until you have recognized it. Or, at the very least, recognized the pain it is causing you by continuing to deny it.

Through My Father's Eyes

Written by C. Simone Rivers
Copyright © 2013

Our relationship was not always what I wanted it to be,
But in the end, I know that he will always be a part of me.
Sometimes I see my yesterday through my father's eyes.

We grew to love and respect each other.
Regardless of our start in this life,
I sometimes see myself through my father's eyes.

He really was a good guy, despite each and every fault.
Like me, he made mistakes but continued to correct his walk.
I can see myself through my father's eyes.

I have children of my own that I love with all my heart.
I think of them often, though we are apart.
I pray that they can see themselves through their father's eyes.

He's transitioned to the next life, and I miss him
oh, so much.
But when I think of him, I smile and still can feel
the touch
Of his hand in our parting embrace.
I see that everything will be just fine
When I'm looking through my father's eyes.

Let it Shine

"I choose to be authentic in everything I do."
~ India Arie ~

As I often do, I was in a store just observing human behavior and enjoying the ways in which we play in the world. I had stopped to grab a few things for my family for dinner, when I ran across a woman and her four children. I surmised that she was a single mom.

There is just something about the demeanor of a single mom. I witnessed those special qualities in my own mother. Single moms have a look that lets you know they don't get much sleep, even though they have mastered the art of napping and firing from all cylinders in spite of it. She is always thinking about tomorrow, and finds it hard to present in the moment. She is highly intuitive. She is conscious of the things her children are not telling her on any given day. She follows her gut and finds her way. She is always in tune with what's going on in her family and always one step ahead.

Oh! A single mom doesn't want anyone feeling sorry for her!

There is no denying she has a lot on her plate, but there is also no denying she is a strong, resourceful, capable, loving mother. Those things and more are what I saw when I observed that woman interacting with her children.

The youngest asked for some things that she told him he could not have. I could tell it wasn't because of nutrition, but merely the means to give him what he wanted. Her eyes told a story of such guilt at having to tell her child "no".

I followed them through the store, making note of each time one of the children asked for something that she was not able or willing to give to them. Once I had a list for all four of the children, I gathered those items and took them to the customer service desk at the front of the store.

I purchased them and asked the manager to give them to the woman and her children. I didn't give her my name, as I didn't want to get any recognition for it. I wanted the items offered to her with dignity, not as if she was a charity case—though charity was certainly the vein of my response. Love and charity are one in the same. I left a note that read, "*God is always watching, and better is waiting for you and your children.*"

After getting the manager to assure me he would not divulge my identity, I stood afar off, waiting to see her reaction. That is what brings me the most joy. The woman smiled and thanked the gentleman. She showed the things to the children, and they were overjoyed. They left the grocery store with a different experience for the day. I just felt that.

There is something about me that is bright. I don't really know what it is, or better still, I don't know how to articulate it. I don't always recognize it. However, throughout my life, people have told me that it exists.

My friend, Jenni, said to me one day that I *"exude so much relevant confidence and speak in such a way, that even the meekest among us feel as though they can grab hold of just a little of that strength right now"*. I am not sure if Jenni knew how much her words lifted me that day, but it speaks to that brightness I hear people say that I have — that bright light that I know I have.

When you experience this life as your authentic self, there is a light that shines from the inside of you. It is the light of the Spirit that illuminates and becomes a beacon for others around you. Your truth offers guidance on the dark days that some might be experiencing. Who you are matters to the world. Don't hide your idiosyncrasies and quirks. Live out loud! Someone is waiting on you!

That's my question for you: Who is waiting on you to show up and bring that shine that is unique to only you? Is it a child looking for direction from a mentor? Is it a colleague contemplating entrepreneurship and looking at your example? Maybe it's an entire people looking for a leader of a movement that will change the lives of many. Perhaps it's a reader waiting to dine on your words. I don't know who it is, but I do know that they are waiting for your goodness and god-ness to show up and show them the way. That's how powerful who you are really is. The light that seeks to express itself through you is brighter when you walk in the truth of who you really are. Let it shine!

"Hope is being able to see that there is light, despite all of the darkness."
~ Desmond Tutu ~

The Target
Written by C. Simone Rivers
Copyright © 2014

No other symbol in history captures and incorporates passion and promise like the cross. Originally, it was two pieces of wood — one vertical, the other horizontal — that branded the eternal hope of glory for the entire world. It conveys a message of what is to come and what life truly is: a cross. Luke 9:23 tells us that we have to take up our cross daily to follow Christ.

The cross is vertical and horizontal, symbolizing our connection to God and our connection to people. Vertical and horizontal connection is both *redemption* and *relationship*. It is *kingdom* and *community*. It's *sanctification* and *service*. I have known many "Christians" in my life. Each of us seems to get either the vertical connection correct or the horizontal connection correct. But it is rare to find someone who is successful at living, speaking, and ministering from where the cross planes intersect. This is the target for all of us.

Friendships come from this place. The love for our spouses, our children, our family, and our friends come from this place. It's that point where he commands of Christ meet. He said to love the

Lord with all your soul and all your mind, but He also said that loving your neighbors was much like the first command. We have to love each other from that heart space where God resides—where the vertical and horizontal intersect, the target. This helps us overlook faults and see people as God sees us.

Always Protect the Head.
~ C. Simone Rivers ~

Can You Hear Me Now?

"That whisper you keep hearing is the universe trying to get your attention."
~ Oprah Winfrey ~

When I was a little girl, I heard my mother talking on the phone. Her voice was in a higher pitch than usual. She was almost singing her words. She had a lovely smile in her voice. She took the time to pronounce her words just right, even when her pronunciations were very wrong. I remember wondering who she was talking to.

When she got off the phone, I asked her, "Mama, who was that on the phone?" She answered, "That was Judy." I wasn't quite courageous enough to ask her why she changed her voice to talk to Ms. Judy. Somehow, I knew even then that questioning my mother about her choice of veneers was not going to turn out well for me. I heard her talk to other people on the phone, and she didn't sound the same.

I found myself wondering why Ms. Judy created a desire in my mother to be 'different'.

As the years went by, I recall being at Ms. Judy's house with my mom more often. At that point, it all made sense to me. The Russell's had a home in Winter Park, Florida on a beautiful lake. It was a big house (by my standards of comparison back then). They had a lot of nice things in their home. It was nicely-furnished and fresh every time I went there. They were obviously in a very different economic class than we were, because our house didn't look like theirs. My mother was a domestic in their home. She was responsible for it being so clean, fresh, and well-presented. I watched her ironing sheets, polishing floors, and scrubbing toilets in their home.

Ms. Judy had children—four girls, from what I can remember now. That is significant to me because it cements in my mind that there were very few differences between Ms. Judy and my mother, but my mom changed when she was around or speaking to Ms. Judy. She expected me to change, too. The problem was that I was unsure who or what she wanted me to change into.

I was taught to be polite, respectful, kind, and not to speak when adults were speaking, so I think I had the behaviors down that my mom wanted me to display. She was very proud of me. She would make a point of telling me that when Ms. Judy was around.

I remember feeling like an accessory sometimes. It wasn't a bad feeling, though. It just felt like I was something my mom put on for the Russell's to make her feel better about herself. Sometimes, it made me feel a little taller, too, that my mom wanted to showcase me to the same woman who caused her to change the octave of her voice and speak differently. I didn't understand *why* it was, but I could acknowledge *that* it was.

The irony of it all is that I began to mimic my mom's voice when she was talking to Ms. Judy. I worked to speak with the right diction all of the time. I became very proper in my communication with nearly everyone. This didn't show up for me on special occasions or for certain individuals. It became *my* voice.

Something about what I heard as a very young, impressionable child helped to create the sound of my soul. I started reading very young. I read book after book so I could share what I'd learned in *my* voice. I was an excellent student and excelled in school because I enjoyed being that accessory of pride that my mother wore.

Now, I think every child thinks this way at one point or another about their caregivers. We seek to pull the light out of others to help us find our way. That's what I was doing with my voice to my mother. It made me happy when she was happy. It made me proud of myself when she was proud of me. I organically found my own voice by eliminating the need to speak anything other than those sounds that brought joy, pride, confidence, and power to those around me. What I have discovered about my own authenticity is that it is in that voice — my voice — that my heart's message is expressed.

It is only then that my truth — my "Self" — can be heard by others. It becomes a spirit of communication that creates the understanding. Scientifically speaking, listening is just the physical activity of sound falling on the ears and the biological processes involved in the perceptions of that sound. Oh, but hearing is the ability and the desire to pay attention to the meaning within the sounds.

Matthew 13:9 says it this way: "He who has ears, let him hear." Now, that was Christ speaking, so I know that He knew everyone there had ears. And if you are not hearing-impaired, you are going to hear. So, what was He saying? Even the disciples asked Him why He spoke in parables. His explanation (from my perspective) was that everyone who listens doesn't actually hear the meaning of the sounds. Everyone who listens doesn't actually understand what it is that is being said.

We listen to the noises in our lives, but we *hear* music. Noise falls on our ears without any effort on our part. Hearing is something you choose to do on a conscious level. Hearing requires concentrations so that the mind processes the sound. So, Jesus was correct. He who has ears, let him hear! No one is barring you from hearing, but outside of your authenticity, you cannot be heard. People will listen, but they will not hear you.

    The tendency for most is to create another sound as they seek to be heard. Unfortunately, they never allow their heart's voice to fall on the ears of others. Soon, after creating so many new voices, they forget what their own actually sounds like.

If you want what you're saying heard, then take your time and say it so that the listener will actually hear it. You might save somebody's life. Your own, first.

~ Maya Angelou ~

The Best

An original work by C. Simone Rivers
Copyright © 2009

The enemy of "best" is the acceptance of others. We write. We sing. We create. That's what artists do within the giftedness with which we each are blessed. There are those who cannot write, who cannot sing, who cannot take *this* and create *that* as well or at all. So, we hear "great job", and we pause en route to "our" best and settle for acceptance of their best — merely good *enough*. My best is mine. It belongs to me. It is not yours. It is not hers. It is not his or theirs. It is mine, but if I decide to stop looking within and choose only to see the perceptions that look around me, over and under me while never seeing inside of me — I am no longer doing "my" best. Instead, I am hoping for *the* best of approvals from others. The best winks and nods or pats on the back from those who cannot climb or even see as high. So, how can they lift me? Imagine how disappointed this makes God. He made you an Everest, and you stopped growing at Blueberry Hill. Perfection is impossible, but excellence is required.

Take It All Off!

"Confidence is the most attractive garment a girl can wear, and authenticity is the shoes and the bag to match."
~ C. Simone Rivers ~

There was a time in my life when I couldn't find anything to love about myself. I hated everything about me. I hated the fact that I was overweight. I hated that I hadn't earned a college degree. I hated the way I looked, spoke, and showed up in the world. I hated my past, my childhood, and my upbringing. I literally hated almost everything about myself. I inherently knew I couldn't go on hating myself that way, so I set out to find a way to love myself.

I started with my fingers. As ridiculous as that sounds, it's true. I have beautiful, long fingers with perfect nail beds. From there, I went to my lips and earlobes. From there, I went to my smile. I looked at my lips and found myself grateful for their perfect shape. I reminded myself of how many women have paid thousands of dollars to get lips that looked like mine.

As preposterous as that sounds, I really had to go to that fundamental extreme to find a path to loving me. I had to strip away all the layers of things I had carried for so many years. You really have to see yourself naked to see your naked Self. You have to strip away all the layers of phony to see divinity within yourself. Self is God, and God lives within each of us.

Remember that Source I talked about earlier? God and Source are, for me, one in the same. We can't see God if we are masking what He made. We are fearfully and wonderfully made, unique expressions of a loving Creator.

Dr. Brene Brown shared in a TED Talk about shame that there is a *"layer of terror that has coated the country"*. We are all asking, "Am I enough? Am I worthy of love and belonging?" She said that the number one casualty of a *"scarcity culture is vulnerability"*. I would go on to say that it is authenticity. I do acknowledge, though, that authenticity requires vulnerability.

Let me share with you in this way: The sunflower is the world's tallest flower, standing up to 30 feet in height. Sunflowers solar-track for maximum energy from the sun. Where the sun goes, so does the sunflower. The scientific term for this "sun-following" habit is heliotropism (and you thought the name came from the way the flower looks). These magnificent plants even self-pollinate. They are remarkable! You will never hear a sunflower say, *"I should be a sunflower"*. It knows what it is *meant* to be. There is no question about it. Under the right conditions, the intrinsic nature of the sunflower seed will emerge and become a sunflower.

The same is true for you and me. It is not a matter of what you *should* be. *"Mom and dad think I should be this or that."* NO! It is about what you are *meant* to be. When you remove the masks that hide who you are, your intrinsic nature can express itself. Just like the sunflower, you will simply "become".

What must you do to create the proper conditions and environment for the emergence of your gifts, talents, skills, and the unique way that the Creator will express through you? That's not rhetorical. Take a moment and answer that question. It will start you on the path toward fulfilling your purpose.

If you are cloaked in something other than your authentic self, you can't really see people and the divinity within them. There is a veil over your eyes that doesn't allow you to see. However, in your authenticity, you can *see* people instead of judging them. You have to strip yourself. You have to be comfortable seeing yourself naked with a knowing that you are perfect (not flawed) and that you are enough. It's when you know you are enough that no matter how others show up, you can love the part of them that you know exists, the divinity in them. We value other people based on the way we value ourselves. So, when we are accepting and loving of ourselves, we can offer the same love and acceptance to others.

The mask? Take it off! Take them all off and look at the masterpiece you've been covering! In case you didn't know, let me just tell you:

You are worthy, necessary, and enough. I want to see more of *you*!

If I had to do it all again (Do Over)

An original work by C. Simone Rivers
Copyright © 2011

If I had to do it all again, of course I'd change some things.
Rearrange some things.
Would I be the same if some things were different?

If I could choose to love again, like way back when, would I choose the same men?
Would I be the same if some things were different?

If I could choose my place again, run the race again, would my pace increase with the thickening of my skin?
Would I be the same if things were different?

If I could be a girl again, swirl and twirl again, would I be happier as a woman or descend again?
Would I be the same if things were different?

I am born again. Saved from sin. He's my friend.
I'm not the same. Things are different.

I have a second chance.

Linked In

"What we are all striving for is authenticity, a spirit-to-spirit connection."

~ Oprah Winfrey ~

For several years, I had a really good friend. One of the greatest things about our relationship was our connection. I knew that he understood me. As a matter-of-fact, I would sometimes get long, detailed letters from him sharing all that was going on in his life, and would sometimes even send the same; and all either of us needed to respond with was one simple word, "connected". We understood each other. Those kinds of relationships are pretty rare in our society, at least in my world. I always say,

"It's better to have four quarters than a hundred pennies!" But what is 'connection'?

To truly connect is to come in contact with the divinity of another person so that the link can be established. We all house divinity. 'Connecting' is recognizing the divinity in another person.

You've heard the term *Namaste*? This is an ancient Sanskrit term still used in daily language in India. The essence of the word is, "*I salute the divinity in you*". I think this is the most beautiful form of a greeting I've heard, and it offers the availability of connection when said to another person.

The connection-contact is more than physical. It's an emotional, spiritual, intellectual contact that establishes a link, or a locking onto divinity with each other. Connection allows for the presence of vulnerability. Vulnerability gives way to authenticity, and the outward and open display of the divinity within us.

My mentor, John Maxwell, says in his book, *Everyone Communicates Few Connect*, that "*connectors create an experience that everyone enjoys"*. I tend to think there is some truth to that. Everyone does, indeed, communicate, but very few people connect to the divinity or "sameness" in others. Instead, we are quick to dismiss people because of the differences.

How many times have you walked past someone and asked how they were, but didn't wait to hear their answer? Sure, you were polite, but you didn't connect with the person.

A few times, I've actually done self-created studies on the way people overlook each other. I went to a mall where there was a critical mass of people. I walked by people and some of them smiled at me and said hello. I also said the same. Then, there were times when someone would say, "Hello! How are you?" I would purposely say, "I feel like I am dying" or "I want to kill myself", or any number of other starling responses. I wasn't heard. I got, "Oh, that's great! Have a nice day!" They never even heard me! It was all route movement through the corridors of life.

Now mind you, I wasn't feeling bad, neither was I contemplating suicide. That experience, though, taught me something. It taught me to listen and be present in the lives of those I encounter. It taught me not to just listen to the words people speak, but to seek to hear their hearts and to salute the divinity in them, no matter the circumstance.

Communication requires connection for it to occur. If you are not living in your authenticity, that true exchange cannot take place. You will find yourself talking at people instead of with them, and vice-versa. However, if you take the time to connect with the common denominator of divinity, you will find that your interactions with people increase in depth and interest. Then what happens? You become one of those connectors that create an experience everyone enjoys!

I have a great story to bring this point to light — one that I watched play itself out in New York City. Remember, I told you I love to people-watch!

I was sitting on a bench on a busy street in the city, just observing those around me. There was a panhandler sitting on the sidewalk as people walked past. Everyone who passed him seemed inconvenienced by his existence. Some people threw money into the bowl he had sitting in front of him. They walked by and just tossed the money in the bowl as if he were a thing or a garbage can they were throwing trash into.

There was one gentleman, though, who walked to the man, gestured, and placed the money in his hand. He looked him in the eye with a nod as if to say, "I see you". I saw a smile adorn the face of the homeless man. His shoulders even squared a bit. I don't know what the homeless man felt in that moment, but I would wager that he was lifted by that simple connection with the divinity in another human being. Someone was actually rooting for his rising! That's what we all want—someone who will root for our rising.

Some people have succumbed to the seduction of social media in that they have replaced real relationships with virtual ones. One Linked In, Facebook, Instagram, Twitter, and YouTube, you have thousands of connections. But do you *really*? Well, in case you were unaware, within social media, you are not *connected* to anyone! You might be communicating, but you are not connecting.

For me, authenticity began with an awareness of who I am. Now, understand this: I don't mean who I am as it relates to the world and the things I do to survive in said world. I am referring to who I am internally; not what I do, but who I *am*. I think for most people, there is never a real need to answer that question. For me, the need presented itself.

You see, my husband moved me from Tampa, Florida to Stuttgart, Germany in the middle of January. I grew up in Florida. It was a part of who I had become. Sunshine ran through my veins! Germany was foreign, both literally and emotionally for me. When I got there, so many parts of who I thought I was were peeled away from me bit by bit. I likened it to a Band-Aid being ripped away…slowly. It hurt like hell! OUCH! Yet underneath, I discovered this big, beautiful, kind, loving, deliciously-fabulous woman. She smiled at me and said hello. I knew we had known each other for years; we'd just lost touch.

I was a mother to my oldest son, Joshua, who had begun to grow up and make choices I was not happy with. So, this layer I called "Super

Mom" was being painfully and slowly peeled away every day for nearly seven years. Now, think about that for a moment. Can you imagine the pain of a Band-Aid being peeled away slowly from the hairs on your arms for seven years of your life? Wouldn't that make you keenly aware of who you are? Surely, it would make you aware of who you wanted to be at the very least, right?

Then there was my marriage and my power. Moving to Germany meant being heaved into a new environment with only one arm of support; my husband. Because of his contract and German law, I wasn't allowed to work, so I had to depend upon him for my love, livelihood, and legitimacy. Wow! That was a painful, frightening place! I needed more from him than he could access and offer. That band-aid started peeling away slowly and painfully — and deliberately exposed me to ME!

Who are you? Do you know who you are? How would you explain yourself to someone you just met without ever saying your name or what you do to make money? What are you here for? What is your unique calling here on earth? What makes you necessary? What is your gift? What is it that you can do that you have always been able to do?

What I know is this: When you are your authentic self, you have a desire to connect with the authenticity of others.

Dressed Up State of Mind

An original work by C. Simone Rivers
Copyright © 2011

I was all messed up. Head reeling with thoughts of "cides". You, me, or the other guy.
Either way, somebody had to die.
Yea, I was all messed up.

Now I'm dressing my wounds with the Balm of Gilead. Jehovah Rapha gave me what I wish I always had.
Yea, I was all messed up.

Where's my little black dress and those Santana shoes?
I'm strutting my stuff, while singing these blues.
Yea, I was all messed up.

But today, I'm in a dressed-up state of mind.

She Can't Read

"Mindfully practicing authenticity during our most soul-searching struggles is how we invite grace, joy, and gratitude into our lives."
~ Brene Brown ~

One day, my friend, Kenneth, and I were at a grocery store in Tampa. We both saw a strikingly beautiful woman. She was perfect! Her waist was snatched and tiny. Her hips and buttocks were perfectly round. Her legs were a cross between a Clydesdale and gazelle. Her hair was cut in a beautiful bob, dusting her shoulders ever-so-gently. Her lips were the lips Chloe Kardashian used to show her plastic surgeon just what she wanted them to look like. Her eyes were big, bright, and gorgeous. Her skin was like a Werther's Original butterscotch candy. She was stunning!

I said to Kenneth, "It's just not fair that God made me this way and she gets to look that way!" (I was well over 200 pounds at the time.) Kenneth looked at me and rather matter-of-factly said, *"She can't read."* He said it with a straight face. *"Believe me. You would rather be able to read than look like that."* I laughed so hard, tears began to flow.

To this day, the memory of that story makes me laugh. Kenneth showed me a few things in his response. The obvious was that comparing myself to others wasn't healthy. He also showed me that my differences are purposeful and that who I am mattered, regardless of who someone else chose to be. Today, I can appreciate what he said so much better.

When you are operating in your own authenticity, you can appreciate the gifts and talents of other people. Competition disappears. Collaboration and celebration become normal.

I can look at other people now and appreciate who they are without it ever diminishing who I am. I am forever grateful for the truth and for the experiences I have had connecting with other people—those I connect with in the grocery store or the mall that I've known for only a moment, and those I have stayed connected to for my lifetime.

I've been in situations when people just didn't like me. There are a multitude of reasons that basically boil down to my having something that they don't. This lack or scarcity mentality creates animosity. My answer to that is gratitude! I am grateful for every intersection I have. I'm grateful for every person I meet and what their divinity will speak to mine, what their authenticity will speak to mine. For me, this required a level of maturity—one I had to grow into. I had to remove my mental self from the environment that taught me I wasn't enough.

We are biologically-wired for survival. Survival is what our brains are thinking every time we get new information, especially information we don't understand. Our brains are wired to protect us, so we create stories that do just that. We will say the pretty girl can't read or whatever other story we need to survive that moment of vulnerability — that moment when pain could be present, lurking, and waiting to attach itself to us...that authentic moment of our very own truth.

However, we will never get to the truth about ourselves or anyone else if we don't allow vulnerability. We have to stop locking the door to it with the head-tales we create that want us to survive some painful, embarrassing moment. We have to allow vulnerability so that we present our authenticity and we can see the divinity in others.

It wasn't until I was able to see myself that I was then able to see other people. It wasn't until I was okay with me that I could appreciate other women and be okay with them as well. Today, I can compliment and lift others without competition or comparison, and recognize that we all have gifts. I have some, and you have some! It was a worthy journey to get to a place where I could appreciate the divinity in other people.

> *"Authenticity helps establish a life of gratitude."*
> ~ C. Simone Rivers ~

My husband snores when he sleeps. I'm not talking about just heavy breathing. This man is calling hogs in his sleep state. Over the years, it has gotten so loud, I often put headphones on, listening to music to drown out the sound of him in order to be able to fall asleep. He snores so loudly, he wakes himself up at times.

I recall a time when he went away on business for a couple of weeks. I found that I missed him, of course. What I missed the most was the sound of him sleeping next to me. That sound let me know he was there, and it offered me comfort, safety, and security. Now, I am truly grateful for his snoring! I still need my earphones sometimes, but I am grateful knowing he is alive and well, right next to me.

The cultivation of gratitude and joy is the path to one's authenticity. When you actively practice gratitude (writing it down), you spend your day in search of it. Gratitude is a tangible thing; it's not abstract. It's not an attitude, but it will *change* your attitude. We spend so much time looking for the big, extraordinary things that we miss the things that are important—those little moments of joyfulness and things we can find to be grateful for in our everyday lives!

Forward

Written by C. Simone Rivers
Copyright 2015

My strong feeling is that you have one of those minds that never rests. You wake up thinking, have constant conversations in your head, coaching yourself, cheerleading yourself, and yes, chastising yourself...often too severely. I also gather from the spirit that there is an ironic guilt because of the many talents you've been given that may not have manifested in visible prosperity. Calm yourself, keep moving, and be patient. The strongest and tallest trees must have the deepest roots. The biggest skyscrapers must be entrenched deep beneath the surface so that they can tower above all. Keep moving forward.

In Living Color

"Presence is more than just being there."
~ Malcolm Forbes ~

Have you ever had a conversation with someone who was either in their past or in their future, but not talking to you right *now*? They are with you in body only, because their thoughts are someplace else. They aren't *present*. Often, they are waiting for you to finish what it is you are saying so that they can say whatever thought it is they want to convey.

When you are operating in authenticity, you are able to be fully present. There is no feeling of missing out on opportunities because someone else is sharing. There is a knowing in you that now matters. You aren't spending a lot of time in the past or projecting into the future. You are present in the *now*. People are able to access your voice and your light in the *now*. You can look people in the eye in your authentic self to make them feel seen *and* heard.

There is a beauty in us all when we just stop for a moment and look. Alice Walker said that it's a sin to walk past the color purple without acknowledging God. I say we all have a rainbow inside of us at any given moment. Sometimes, it's red with anger and passion. Sometimes, it's yellow because we want to offer friendship to other people. Other times, it's green because we are feeling prosperous and helping others get there, too.

You can't be present when you are pretending you are someone else and spending too much time trying to make sure your mask is on properly.

I recall Oprah Winfrey saying many times on her show that people just want to know they are being heard. My son comes to mind.

When I have a conversation with him, I look him in the eyes and listen to him. I want him to know he is being heard. If he is talking to me and I'm in the middle of something else, I will ask him if he minds me not giving him my full attention. People call multitasking a 'thing'. I think it is a joke, because you can't split your energy and be fully present.

When you are authentic, you are fully present and your energy is focused. Your light is shining on one person, place, or thing. Your conversation naturally lifts in esteem, and you become the connector that offers an experience everyone enjoys.

When you are showing up in the world as who you really are, you experience life in the moment. You are able to be present and enjoy life moment by moment. You realize that right now is all you really have. You don't spend a lot of time brewing over the past or looking forward to the future. You eat an apple and enjoy, right now. You have a conversation and participate in it, right now. Sex, for instance, is at its best when you are experiencing it in the present moment.

As you are reading this chapter, I am launching my book at Village Connector Studio in Laurel, MD. I wanted to share with you a moment I had living in full out color.

I met a beautiful young lady who had her own television show. Our encounter, though new, was so genuinely authentic. She was of "like tribe" if you will. We became instant compadres. I know that I was nervous about the launch and the show (look for it on my YouTube channel, Deliciously Fabulous TV), but her "realness" gave me permission to stay in the moment and share the truth of what I was feeling and what my intentions were. It was a wonderful experience that I catalog in the library of my mind.

"Stress is caused by being 'here' and wanting to be 'there'."
~ Eckart Tolle ~

RESPONSIBILITY
Written by C. Simone Rivers
Copyright © 2011

Little feet following me everywhere I go.
Little minds asking me everything I know.
Little hands doing what they see me do.
Little feet, little mind, little hands.
Grown man for some little one to follow now.

Lifeline

"An authentic life is the most sincere form of worship."
~ Sarah Ban Breathnach ~

L et's go back to Silke. When you are operating in your authentic self, all of the following things come into play:

✞ *You have power from the Source that is always present.*
✞ *You are a light that shines for others to find their way.*
✞ *You can be heard, and your voice is like music that encourages others' lives to dance.*
✞ *You can connect with the divinity of other people, and you can appreciate the truth about them and*

yourself, and you know that we are all unique expressions of a loving Creator.
- *You can see your 'Self', which makes it so much easier to see others.*
- *Your color…your rainbow shows that pot of gold at the end of it, and you might actually save someone's life, because they didn't have that connection to life that only you could provide them.*

"Nature is infinitely creative. It is always producing the possibility of new beginnings."

~ *Marianne Williamson* ~

Recently, I was talking to a friend of mine who complimented my hair. I said "thank you" and also shared that it was a wig. He was upset with me. He questioned my authenticity based on that knowledge. I went on to tell him that my natural hair is really hard to deal with. I love it, but it takes a considerable amount of work to be glamorous every day. Our meeting was spur-of-the-moment, and I didn't have time to wash, twist, dry-set, and stretch my hair! So, in a clutch, I popped on a wig that looked just like my hair and kept it moving.

Why am I sharing this with you? Because I am sure there are some others out there who make the mistake of thinking authenticity is something you put on or take off. It is not! It is who you *are*.

No matter what I choose to do to my hair — put on the wig or shave my head even — my authenticity is not suddenly stripped away. Authenticity is showing up in your truth. It's genuine, trustworthy, and bona fide YOU! It's your heart, your spirit, your emotions, and your conscious connections with others.

It was William Shakespeare who said, "*To thine own self be true, and it must follow, as the day to the night, thou canst not be false to any man*". So, being true to self will create the way you show up to others. Good, old William gave some good advice!

When I examined my life, and looked for the truth of who I really am, I had to go through layers and layers of labels. I found that each one of them were less about me and more about the person or persons that benefited from them. I am a wife to my husband. I am a mother to my children. I am a friend to so many. I am a Christian to those who need me to show up that way, but I am just spiritual for those who didn't want that identity to stick. I found that I could use race, gender, body size, body type, religion, political party, or a host of other things that had been given to me. They were not who I am! What I realized was that I was looking externally to find out who I was, and that was a problem.

Social media (and media in general), along with all of the fake reality television shows, seeks to push us towards identifying ourselves based on their need for fame and fortune. What I have found to be true for myself and everyone I meet is that authenticity is decreasing and ultimately eliminating the gap that is present between who we know we are deep down inside and what we actually disclose to the world around us. Authenticity requires courage!

It doesn't matter how you look—big or small, short or tall, black or white, rich or poor.

When you are able to operate in the world as your authentic self, there are a few things that happen. You become more powerful than you ever could know. There is this seed inside of all of us, put there by our Source (God). It is the seed of divinity that we often call *potential*.

There is a law of reciprocity that says, "You reap what you sow", but that is not the whole story. You don't just reap what you sow. You reap more than you sow, and you reap much longer than you've sown. So, that seed inside of you has the ability to become a tree or even a forest.

These seeds whisper every now and again. You have to listen for them. The noise of "*I should be*" and the masks we have learned to wear make it hard to hear their sound of the seeds of potential. I promise you. If you would just listen, you will hear that seed inside of you calling you back to the truth of who you really are. That seed wants to be watered and nurtured so that it can grow. They call us back to ourselves. Some of us were meant to be forests. Some of us were meant to be flowers. Some of us were meant to be gardens. *None* of us were meant to remain a seed!

Yet, how many of us die with that seed still there, never having been allowed to grow?

When you mask the truth of who you are, you cannot tap into the power of your potential. Your authenticity exposes your purpose. It was Mark Twain who said, *"The two most important days in a person's life are the day you were born and the day you figure out why"*. Your purpose is your 'why'. You discover your 'why' because of courage—the courage to be vulnerable. You cannot access your authenticity without vulnerability.

Note: Courage is not the absence of fear. Courage is a decision to do it afraid.

At the end of vulnerability is courage and the cornerstone of confidence. So, have the courage to be vulnerable, showing the world who you really are. You will discover your 'why' and the 'how' of it will just show up! It may show up in a book you write. It may show itself in the kids you mentor or the friendships you build. However, until you take off the mask and operate in your own authenticity, your purpose will remain hidden.

After you have accessed your power and discovered your purpose, in your authenticity, you will attract a certain kind of people. People who were placed here to water your potential and nurture that seed inside of all of us. People who build and lift you up to the top of your specific life's mountain. There, you will find all of the possibilities for your life.

Refuse to let people tell you who you are supposed to be. Don't let anyone tell you how big or small you can be, how loud your voice can be, or how bright your light can be. Listen to the voice of that seed on the inside. Nurture it with possibility. You just might discover you have the potential to be an Oprah Winfrey or Stevie Wonder! You might discover you have the seed to produce a life like Number 44, our beloved former President Barack Obama. Or to make a difference to a team like Larry Bird did with the Celtics.

It could also be that you grow to be a 16-year-old girl named Sydnee, born with Down Syndrome, who teaches me what unconditional love looks like every single time I see her. Maybe you are that stay-at-home mom who chose to raise her children to be awesome members of society. You see, no one is more valuable than the other. We are all unique expressions of a loving Creator. Every one of us matters to the world.

Who YOU are matters. What you were given to offer the world is so valuable. If you don't feed me what God gave you just for me, I die hungry. You have a responsibility to live up to your potential. Take off the mask. Quit shrinking to let others feel bigger. Let your light shine and know that you will never cast a shadow on anyone else. In fact, you become a beacon that guides others toward letting their light shine, too! In the becoming of who you really are, you just might get an opportunity like I did; to save someone's life.

Your Authenticity Matters.

"When you are content to be simply yourself and don't compare or compete, everybody will respect you."
~ Lao Tzu ~

Random Thought That Offers Guidance
Written by C. Simone Rivers
Copyright © 2017

Wouldn't you 'put up your dukes' and enter the ring if you knew the fight was fixed and winning was guaranteed, even if it's a Mike Tyson-like opponent? Well, that is the truth about this life.

God gives us the sight, the right, and the might to do great things. Don't miss this! We just have to develop the fight!

What is Sight? He gives us vision, goals, desires even in the midst of storms. Sight is what you want for yourself.

What is your Right? The fact that Christ died gives you an all-access pass to every good thing.

What is Might? This is your strength to carry everything your life offers to the finish line.

Now, what is your job? Your job is to fight. Faith is the muscle that supports your fight.

Now, you know. Go and be awesome!

Epilogue

"Maybe the journey isn't so much about becoming anything. Maybe it's about unbecoming everything that isn't really you, so you can be who you were meant to be in the first place."

~ Unknown ~

When I was a little girl, I was playing with a neighborhood friend, Regina. We had each been given helium-filled balloons with strings tied to them for us to hold onto and keep them from flying away. On our balloons, we wrote in black magic marker (that's pre-Sharpie language for you young folk) our names and what we wanted to be famous for when we grew up. I was going to be a writer and talk to people all around the world. (I can't remember what Regina was going to be. I think he wanted to dance.) I have always wanted to write, and I wanted people to hear the things I felt rising up inside of me to say.

Regina and I let go of our balloons, thinking they would float up to Heaven, God would read what we wanted to be, and make it come true. Well, Regina's balloon went up really, really high. After a while, we couldn't see it anymore. I just knew her balloon made it to God. When I let my balloon go, it went up and got caught in a tree. It was too high for me to reach, and it just sat there…stuck.

I remember being so upset. I started mocking the balloon. *"You stupid balloon! I hate you!"* I hated my balloon because it didn't go as high as Regina's balloon. Her balloon "worked". Mine didn't.

That is how some of us might look at our lives. I'm telling you that your authenticity matters — who you are matters to the world — but you are stuck. Your "tree" might be the environment you grew up in and the voices of your parents. You might have gotten stuck because of some early choices you made. You might have gotten stuck because you chose to do what someone else wanted you to do with your career, instead of following your passion. Perhaps you got married, had children, and found yourself stuck because of it. You look at the other people around you ascending in their lives, and it makes you questions the value of your balloon.

You begin to hate your balloon because it doesn't look like someone else's balloon. You begin to hate your life because it doesn't look like someone else's life. You close your book because your story doesn't seem as interesting as someone else's story.

Listen! Where, when, or even how you got stuck doesn't matter. This is what I want you to know: There is nothing fundamentally wrong with your balloon. There is nothing inherently wrong with your life. You can ascend as high as you believe you can. Your story is one that people are waiting to hear. You have to let go of the limiting beliefs — the B.S. (Belief System) that created the things you got stuck on in the first place.

Know that you are enough. Watch your balloon start to rise up and create exactly what you were meant to bring to this world. I don't know what that specific thing is for you, but I know it matters.

I know that YOU matter!

Your Authenticity Matters. Now, let it rise!

SAYING GOODBYE
Written by C. Simone Rivers
Copyright © 2011

I was hurt. I am healing.
I was angry. I now have peace.
I forgave. I will never forget.
I once loved you more than I loved myself.
Now, I understand my own mistakes.
I love God, so I cannot hate you.
My circle opened just wide enough for you to step out.
You are no longer welcome around my heart.
Take good care,
Simone

APPENDIX

Angelou, M. (n.d.) Quote retrieved from https://www.brainyquote.com/quotes/quotes/m/mayaangelo634487.html

Beckwith, M. B. (2016). *Michael Bernard Beckwith's Prayer for When You're Feeling Stuck.* SuperSoul Sunday. OWN. Retrieved from https://www.youtube.com/watch?v=5hTOXoMrNd4

Brown, B. (2012). *Listening to Shame.* TED Talks TV via YouTube. Retrieved from https://www.youtube.com/watch?v=psN1DORYYV0

Maxwell, J.C. (2010). *Everyone Communicates, Few Connect.* Thomas Nelson Publishers / HarperCollins Publishers, Nashville, TN.

Tutu, D. (n.d.) Quote retrieved from https://www.brainyquote.com/quotes/quotes/d/desmondtut454129.html

Winfrey, O. (n.d.) Quote retrieved from https://quotefancy.com/quote/879543/Oprah-Winfrey-That-whisper-you-keep-hearing-is-the-universe-trying-to-get-your-attention

ACKNOWLEDGMENTS

To my mom, Blanche Goddard: Who I am and who I will become is because of who you chose to be — my mother. I love you.

Thank you, Floyd Smith with FS Dezigns LLC, for designing my book cover. Your kindness in the midst of my storm is so appreciated. www.fsdezigns.com 727-846-3487

I would like to thank my sister-friend, Nosa Owens, for always believing in me and for showing me just how much authenticity matters in friendship. Don't ever change.

To my beautiful friends in Germany - Bettina, the Seume family, and the Woerle family: Your culture and country were the birthplace for this work. Thank you for welcoming me in and loving who I really am.

Will Crawford, thank you for your ear at a time when I needed it most. Yours was the push I needed to take the first step.

To Remedy, thanks for lying to me. It was in pursuit of my own truth that I discovered the most beautiful parts of myself.

Thank you to my Deliciously Fabulous Tribe, the Influence community, all of my Facebook friends, my Instagram contacts, and my Twitter people. Your likes, comments, and shares of my thoughts continue to propel me forward.

WHAT OTHERS ARE SAYING...

"Simone is a ball of positive energy. She loves to pour into others. It's hard not to be drawn to her."

~ Keisha Boyd, Owner/Pickett PR Group

****

"Simone is a light in the darkness. She speaks with a prophetic voice and calls to the deep within those who need to hear a message of hope, courage, and empowerment."

~ Shawn Douglass, MindShift Mentor

****

"...the epitome of confidence lived out loud. This fun, loving, and beautiful woman is an inspiration to anyone who feels disenchanted, disqualified, or disconnected."

~ Michelle Belcher

****

"When Simone puts pen to paper, it becomes a work of art! A strong, beautiful, and intelligent sister, with an incredible way of drawing you in with rich images of life experiences and her love and passion for helping people because Authenticity absolutely matters!"

~ Harriett Loney, iSpark Transformation, LLC

****

"C. Simone Rivers is a force of nature that will shake you out of your slumber and cause you to awake the greatness within. Authenticity Matters is a must-read for anyone and everyone that desires to have their original, undiluted individuality be seen in the world."

~ R. Marc Thompson, Jr.

****

"When I think of Simone, I know that nothing is impossible because she encourages everyone to be the best versions of themselves. I witness her set her goals, go through ups and downs, and accomplish her goals. Simone always tells the truth about a situation, and she encourages people by lifting them. After reading her words, I'm left in tears because her beautiful spirit encourages me. I hope that everyone has a Simone in their life."

~ **Natasha M. Hinds, Co-Founder, Keep Your Hair Headgear, LLC**

ABOUT THE AUTHOR

C. Simone Rivers is President and Chief Imagination Officer of Deliciously Fabulous, LLC — a personal development services consultancy. She is an International Speaker and Trainer focused on personal empowerment, productivity, and closing performance gaps.

Simone is known as the Yum-Yum Ambassador because she influences the flavor in the room. Things are always good after she arrives.

A member of the Possibilities Syndicate, Simone addresses and impacts audiences internationally and is recognized, by clients and peers alike, for her ability to expand awareness from what *is* to what is *possible*.

Simone is certified in the leadership philosophy of John C. Maxwell — the world's #1 leadership expert. While personal development is her passion, professional development is a part of the meat and potatoes of her business.

Having lived and worked on three continents, Simone has birthed a distinctive flavor in her delivery that is compelling to audiences of various cultural backgrounds. She is not a travel agent sending people to places she has never been herself. She is, instead, a tour guide, offering first-hand knowledge and experience to guide her audiences in their transformation.

C. Simone Rivers currently resides in the DC metropolitan area with Victor, her husband of 17 years. She is the proud mother of two boys (Joshua 22 and Jameson 14) and enjoys learning in all forms, mentoring young girls, fishing, and living life as loudly as possible.

To bring Simone's influence to your organization, club or women's group, please call 813-569-0725 or we encourage you to send an email to Simone@deliciouslyfabulous.com.

Simone will be doing an International Virtual Book Tour in select cities. If you are interested in bringing her to your city, please call the number above. There are also "Chat-n-Chill with Simone" events available for your clubs and organizations. To create this unique event for your audience, please visit the website at www.deliciouslyfabulous.com.

Thank you.

www.ingramcontent.com/pod-product-compliance
Lightning Source LLC
Chambersburg PA
CBHW071530080526
44588CB00011B/1628